New Millennium Voice Series

GRADE ONE

Editorial Committee
D.F. Cook
Elizabeth Parsons
Anita Ruthig

With thanks to Lisa Martin, Jennifer Floris, and Debra Wanless for their assistance.

Official Examination Repertoire List Pieces and Studies of Conservatory Canada - Grade 1

Publication of the New Millennium Voice Series is made possible by a generous grant from Dr. Don Wright.

ISBN 978-0-88909-187-0

Novus Via Music Group Inc.
189 Douglas Street, Stratford, Ontario, Canada N5A 5P8
(519) 273-7520 www.NVmusicgroup.com

‹r design:
‹in E. Cook, AOCA

About the Series

The *New Millennium Voice Series* is the official repertoire for Conservatory Canada examinations. This graded series, in eight volumes (Grade 1 to Grade 8), is designed not only to serve the needs of teachers and students for examinations, but it is also a valuable teaching resource and comprehensive anthology for any singer. The List Pieces have been carefully selected and edited, and represent repertoire from the Baroque, Classical, Romantic/Impressionist, and 20th-century periods. In addition, each volume includes the syllabus requirements for the grade, a graded arrangement of *O Canada* (with words in English and French), and a Glossary containing a short biography of each composer. Conservatory Canada requires that at least one Canadian composition be performed in every examination. Composers working in Canada are well represented in the series. A small asterisk next to their name identifies them. Photographs of some Canadian composers are included with the biography.

Notes on Editing

Most composers in the Baroque and Classical periods included only sparse dynamic, articulation, tempo and other performance indications in their scores. Where we felt it necessary, we have added suggested markings. The *New Millennium Series* is not an Urtext edition. All editorial markings are intended to be helpful suggestions rather than a final authority. The choice of tempo is a matter of personal taste, technical ability, and appropriateness of style. Most of our suggested metronome markings are expressed within a range of tempi. In the 19th and 20th centuries, composers included more performance indications in their scores, and as a consequence, fewer editorial markings have been required.

No markings have been used to suggest phrasing and breathing. In accordance with Conservatory Canada's policy regarding redundant accidentals, we have followed the practice that a barline cancels accidentals. Unnecessary accidentals following the barline have been used only in exceptional circumstances.

Bearing in mind acceptable performance practices, you are free to use your own judgement, musicianship and imagination in changing any editorial marking, especially in the areas of dynamics, articulation, and phrasing.

Every effort has been made to identify the authorship of texts and translations. Where we have not been able to confirm that the authorship is generally accepted as being anonymous, we have used the term "unknown". In the matter

The pieces in the *New Millennium Series* have been chosen as an introduction to enjoyable repertoire that is fun to sing while, at the same time, helps to develop your technique and musicianship. We hope you will explore the broad variety of styles and periods represented in this book. It is important that you learn as many pieces as possible before deciding which ones you will sing in the examination.

London, Ontario
September 1999

The Conservatory Canada Voice Syllabus gives full details regarding examinations. Teachers, students, and parents are advised to consult the most recent Syllabus for current requirements, regulations, procedures and deadline for application.

Table of Contents

A CHILD'S PRAYER

Constance Barbour

*W.H. Anderson
(1882-1955)

10
mf
where.
Heav'n - ly Fa - ther, Thou hast
mp
mf
13
giv - en Me my life and joy - ful heart.
16
p
May they al - ways be, O Fa - ther, For Thy us - ing set a -
p

19
mp
part.
Dear - est Friend of lit - tle chil - dren,
p

22
Look - ing on me from a - bove.
Take the prayer I of - fer
p

25
rall. e dim.
to Thee, Take my lit - tle prayer of love.
rall. e dim.

MRS. DINOSAUR

Clifford Crawley

*Clifford Crawley
(1929-)

Largamente ♩ = 69-76

mf

f ten. ten. mp

1. Mis-sus Di-no-saur was a migh-ty crea-ture. (Though we nev-er knew her per-son-al-ly), Her size was a lit-tle ov-er power-ing And from what re-mains is was

was n't no-ted for her brain power, There's no doubt that she was ve-ry strong, A real hu-mung-ous la-dy, Who was hea-vy, tall, and

4

7

10
plain to see That she was - n't ex - act - ly___ glam - our - ous, And,___
wide and long. If you'd ev - er met Mis - sus___ Di - no - saur Ma - ny
13
jud - ging from what we're_ told, Her tem - per was a lit - tle un -
dif - f'ren - ces would a - rise, I think that there is lit - tle we'd a -
16
cer - tain, And her man - ner just a lit - tle too bold.
gree on, And it is - n't just a ques - tion of size.
f
ten.

19
1.
mf
2.
f
2. Though she
3. Yes, Mis - sus
Di - no - saur was a migh - ty
ten.
ten.
mf
22
la - dy,
(Mis - ter
Di - no - saur was ve - ry big
too),
It's
mp
25
good that her fam - i - ly
be - came
ex - tinct
long be - fore the
time
cresc.
28
of
me
and
you!
ff
ten.

SOMEONE

Walter de la Mare

*Violet Arche
(1913-

Andantino ♩ = 88-96

mf

Some - one came knock - ing at my

p

mf

5

wee small door. Some - one came knock - ing I'm sure, sure, sure; I

8

list - ened, I o - pened, I looked to left and right. But nought there was a stir - ring in the

1
rit.
mf a tempo
still dark night. On - ly the bu - sy beet - le tap - tap - ping on the wall.
rit.
pp
mf a tempo
5
broadly
f
mf
On - ly from the for - est the screech - owl's call. On - ly the crick - et whist - ling
broadly
f
mf
8
rit.
when the dew drops fall, so I know not who came knock - ing, At all, at all, at all.
rit.

RABBITS

W.H. Belyea

*W.H. Bely
(1917-

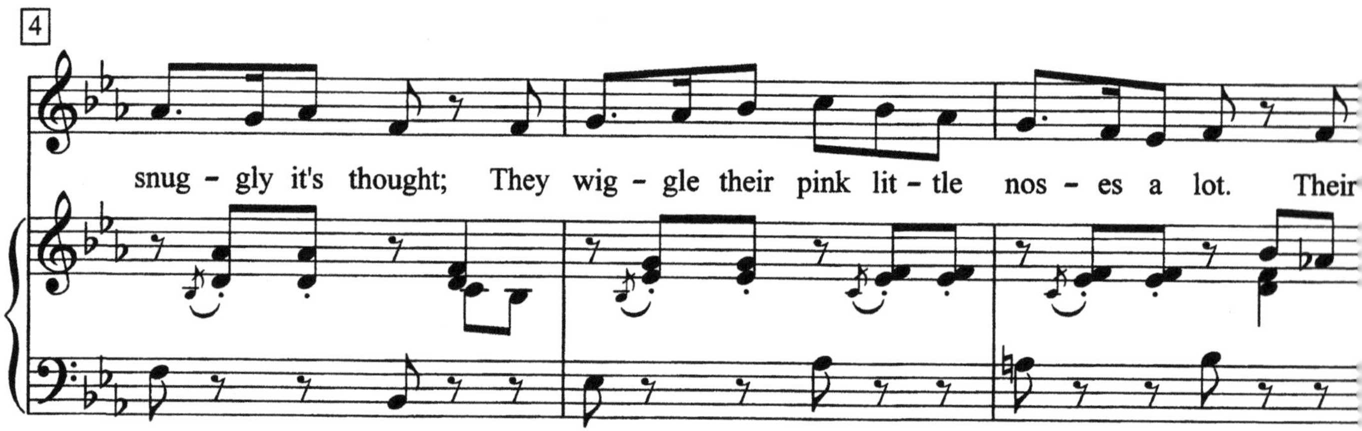

front are so tall! They slow-ly go hip-pit-y
mp
mf
hop-ping a-round; But when they are fright-ened they're off with a bound. I
rall.
a tempo
guess that is why mum-my says it's my hab-it When work's to be done, to take
off like a rab-bit!
f
accel.

MY CATERPILLAR

Marilyn E. Broughton

*Marilyn E. Broughto
(1940-

13
eyes were big like beads, and his coat was ve - ry fur - ry. He
mf
17
mp
had so ma - ny ti - ny legs and yet he did not hur - ry. I
mp
21
put my fin - ger in his way. He crawled up with a wrig - gle. His
p

25
mf
fur was tick - lish on__ my skin and made_ me near - ly gig - gle. Th
mp
mf

29
f
more he crawled up - on my hand, the more tick - lish I___ be -
f

32
mf
rit.
p
meno rit.
came. I fi - nal - ly had to let__ him go, al - though he was quit
mf
rit.
p
meno rit.

tempo primo
mf
tame. I watched my craw - ly crea - ture go cree - ping a - way from
tempo primo
mp
f
me. "I'll play with you a - no - ther day," I
mp
f
mp
pp
called. "Just wait_ and see. Just wait_ and see. Just wait_ and see."

ONE AUTUMN DAY

Margaret Rose

Thomas F. Dunh
(1877-194

Brightly ♩ = 76-88

p

When I went out one
When I went out one

mp

p

4

Aut - umn day I heard a swal - low call - ing
Aut - umn day I heard a swal - low sing - ing

7

mp

"Come lit - tle bro - thers, we must fly, For see, the leaves are
"Sing, lit - tle bro - thers, sing good - bye, Be - fore we all go

mp

fall - ing!
wing - ing.
Spread out your wings and fol - low me," He called to all the
oth - ers, "I'll lead the way a - cross the sea, Come
quick-ly lit-tle bro-thers."
4
8

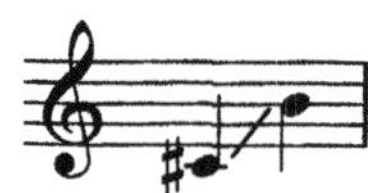

SUMMER LULLABY

from *If You Ever Meet a Dinosaur*

Unknown

Camilla Duri
(20th Centu

Dreamily ♩ = 80-92

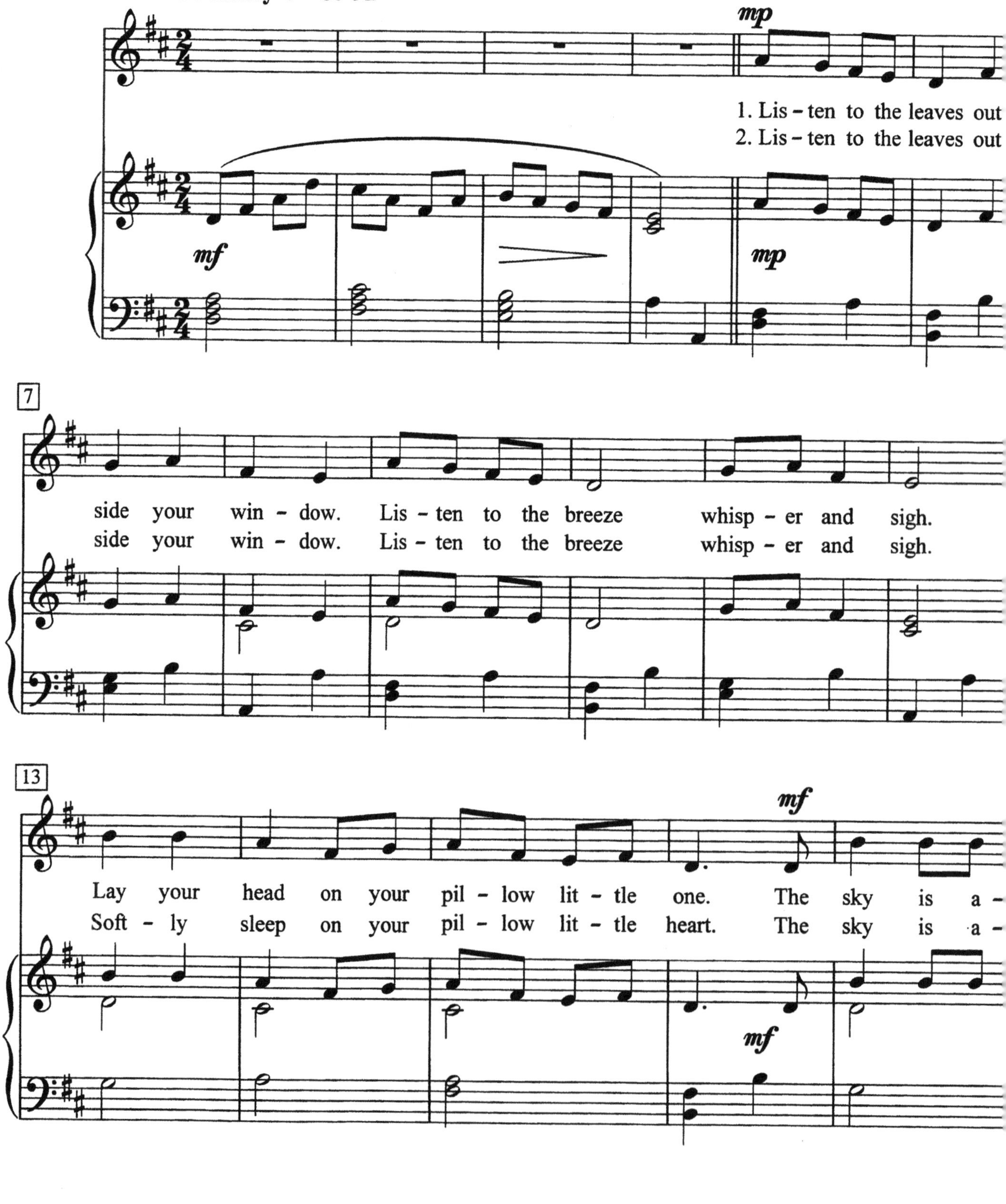
mp
1. Lis - ten to the leaves out
2. Lis - ten to the leaves out
mf
mp
7
side your win - dow. Lis - ten to the breeze whisp - er and sigh.
side your win - dow. Lis - ten to the breeze whisp - er and sigh.
13
mf
Lay your head on your pil - low lit - tle one. The sky is a -
Soft - ly sleep on your pil - low lit - tle heart. The sky is a -
mf

mp
glow with the set - ting sun. All the wea - ry birds are
light with the twink - ling stars. All your sleep - y friends are
mp
nest - ling for the night. Their songs will wake you in the morn - ing
rest - ing for the night. They will call you in the morn - ing
8
mp
poco rit.
D.C.
light. Their songs will wake you in the morn - ing light.
light. They will call you in the morn - ing light.
D.C.
poco rit.

THE SNOWMAN

Unknown

Traditio
arr. D.F. Co

Lively ♩ = 104-116

mp mf

3

mf

1. Once a jol - ly snow - man stood out - side the door,
2. So he called the north wind: "Help me, wind, I pray,

mp

5

Thought he'd like to come in - side and play__ on the floor,
I'm com - plete - ly fro - zen stand - ing here__ all__ day."

Thought he'd like to warm him - self by the fire red,
So the north wind came a - long and blew him in the door.
1.
mf
Thought he'd like to climb up - on the big white bed.
1.
2.
molto rall.
mp
Now there's no - thing left of him but a pud - dle on the floor.
2.
molto rall.
p
8vb

GRANDFATHER CLOCK

Margaret Rose

Thomas F. Dun[illegible]
(1877-19[illegible]

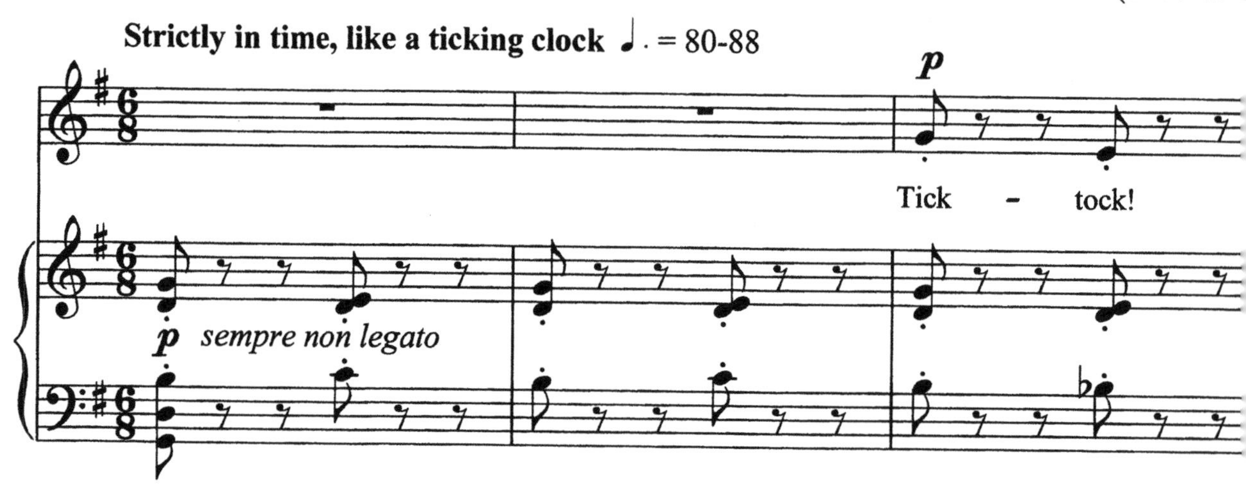

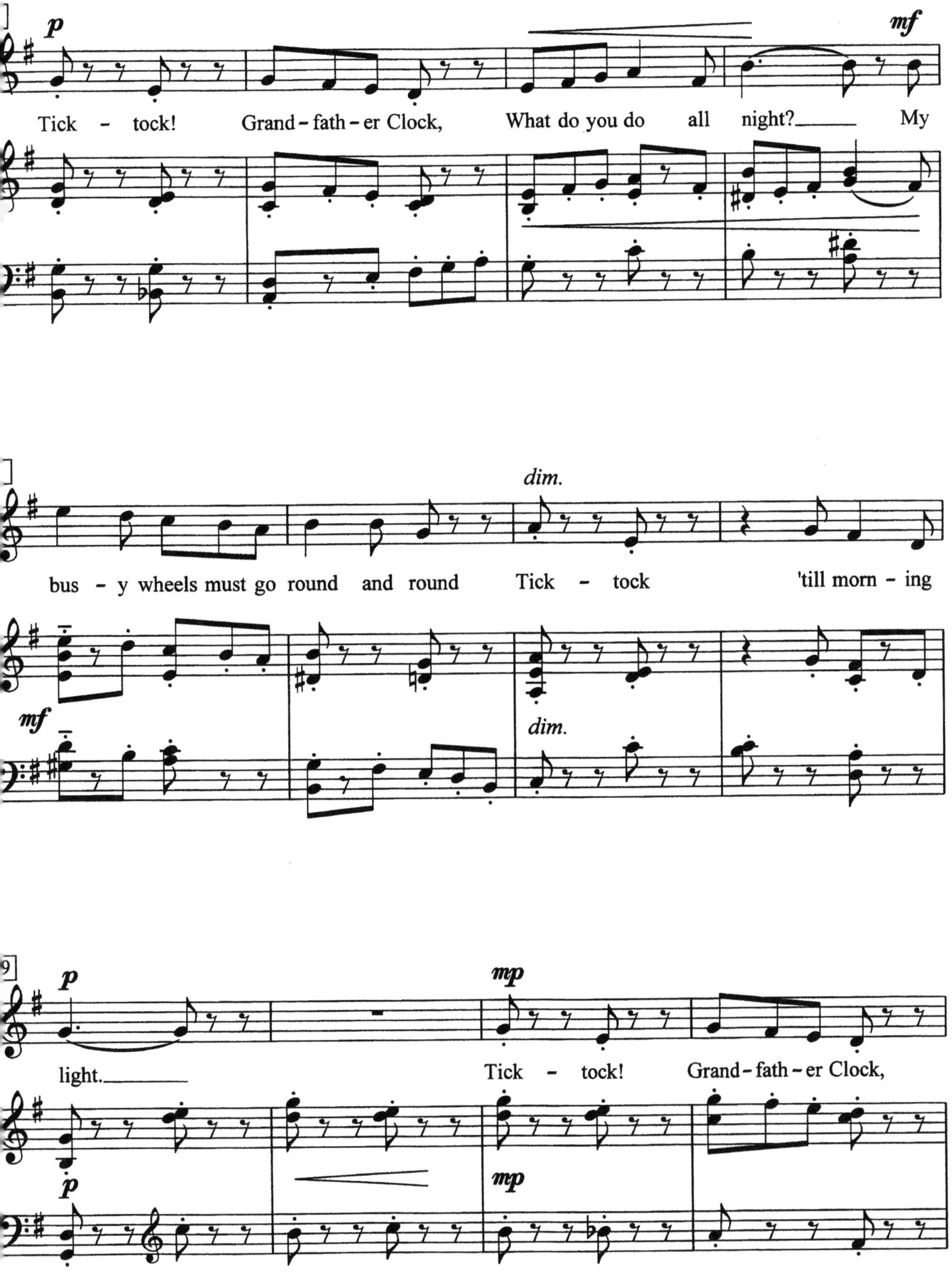

p *mf*

Tick - tock! Grand - fath - er Clock, What do you do all night? My

mf *dim.*

bus - y wheels must go round and round Tick - tock 'till morn - ing

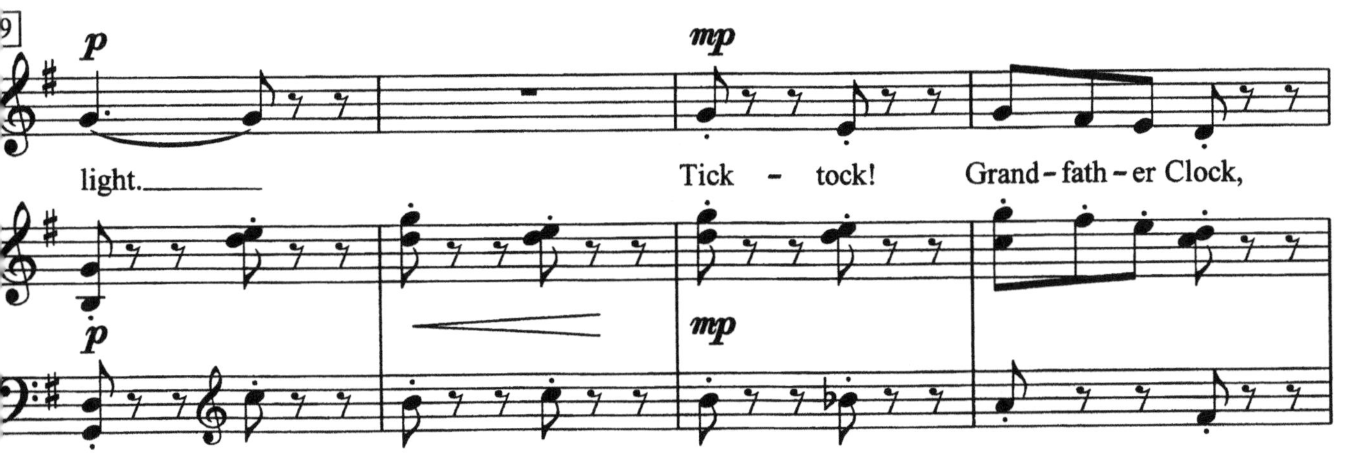

23
mf
Say do you nev - er stop? I work by night and I work by day
mf

27
mp
mf
p
Tick - tock! Tick - tock! Tick -
p
poco cresc.

31
tock!
senza rit.
pp
ppp

SNOW

nymous
rse 3 by Gordon M. Fleming)

*Gordon M. Fleming
(1903-1959)

Gently, but happily ♩. = 66-76

1. Oh when the snow falls down at night and makes the mor - ning still and white; With not a foot - print you can see, There's no - one in the world but me.
2. But then the snow - plow - man I hear, He's scrap - ing all the road - ways clear. I must get up; this is the day When ev - ery one goes out to play.
3. I'll jump in - to the big - gest drift, Then roll a ball too big to lift, Then build a fort a met - re high And hide when all the snow balls fly.

rit.

L.H.

ACADIAN LULLABY

Anonymous
English version by D. F. Cook

*Canadian Folks
arr. Roberta Step

Gently 𝅗𝅥 = 46-52

mp

Dors, dors, le p'tit bi - bi,
Sleep, sleep, my lit - tle child,

5

C'est le beau p'tit bi - bi à ma - ma. Dors, dors,
You are mo - ther's___ beau - ti - ful babe. Sleep, sleep,

8

dors, dors, Dors, dors le bi - bi à ma - ma.
sleep, sleep, Sleep, sleep my___ beau - ti - ful babe. To

cresc.
De - main s'y fait beau j'i - rons au grand - père, Dors___ dors, le
mor - row if it's fine we will see grand - dad. Sleep,___ sleep, my
cresc.
mp
p'tit bi - bi, Dors, dors, dors, dors,
lit - tle child. Sleep, sleep, sleep, sleep,
Dors le beau p'tit bi - bi à ma - ma.
Sleep,_ sleep my___ beau - ti - ful babe.
rit.
pp

J'ENTENDS LE MOULIN

I Hear the Mill-Wheel

Traditional (Québec)
English version by Edith F. Fowke

*Canadian Folk Sc
arr. Stephen Fiel

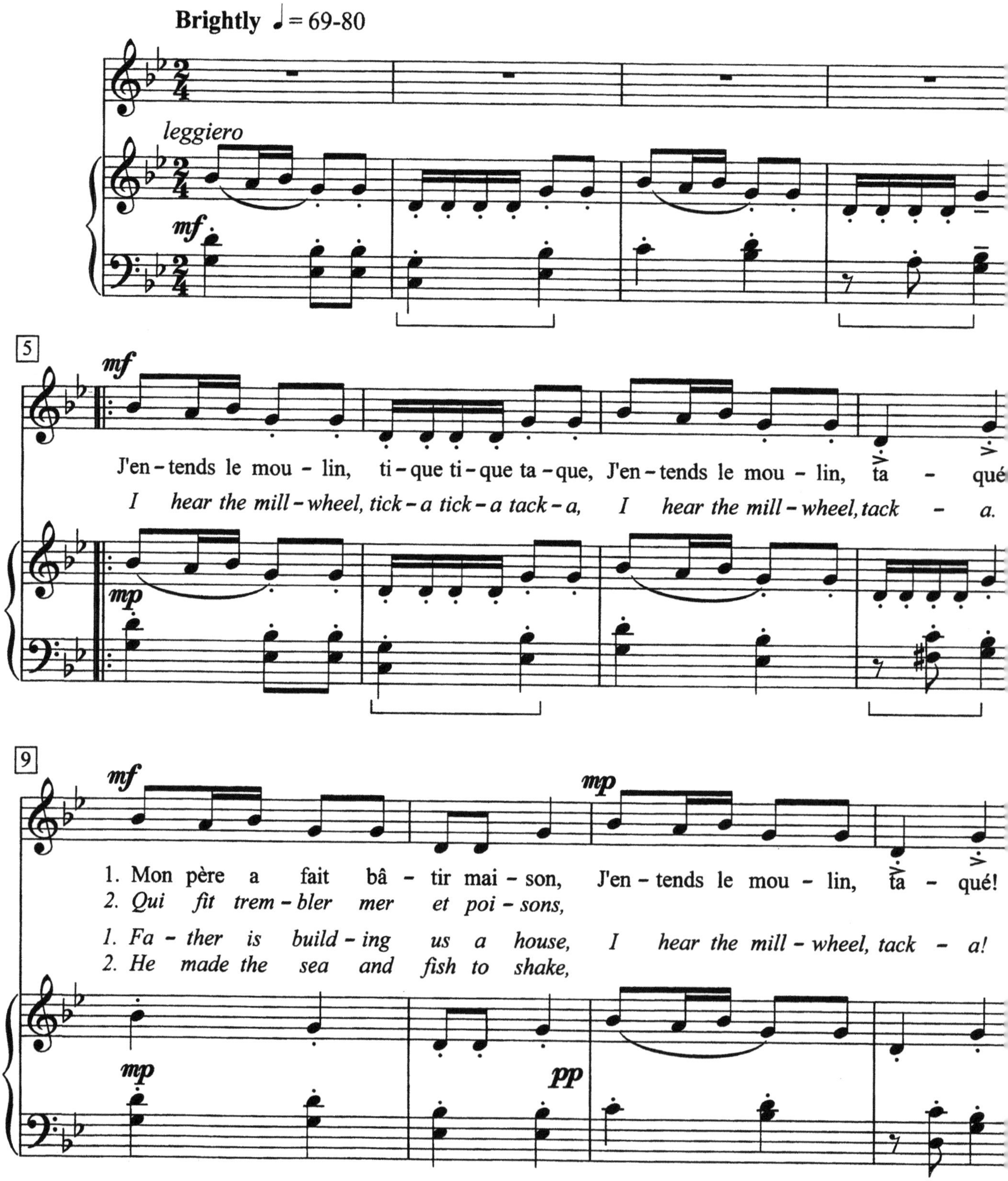

Brightly ♩ = 69-80

leggiero

5

J'en - tends le mou - lin, ti - que ti - que ta - que, J'en - tends le mou - lin, ta - qué
I hear the mill - wheel, tick - a tick - a tack - a, I hear the mill - wheel, tack - a.

9

1. Mon père a fait bâ - tir mai - son, J'en - tends le mou - lin, ta - qué!
2. Qui fit trem - bler mer et poi - sons,

1. Fa - ther is build - ing us a house, I hear the mill - wheel, tack - a!
2. He made the sea and fish to shake,

13
mf
poco rit.
L'a fait bâ - tir à trois pi - gnons, ti - que ta - que, ti - que
Et les cail - loux qui sont au fond,
Car - pen - ters three work on his house, tick - a tack - a tick - a
Al - so the peb - bles in the lake,
mp
poco rit.
16
mf
a tempo
ta - que. J'en - tends le mou - lin, ti - que ti - que ta - que,
tack - a. I hear the mill - wheel, tick - a tick - a tack - a,
mp
a tempo
19
J'en - tends le mou - lin ta - qué.
I hear the mill - wheel, tack - a!
pp

SAKURA

Cherry Blossom

Traditional (Japan)

Japanese Folk Son

arr. G. Brac

13
Flow - ers of the cher - ry__ tree,
Yo - shi - na at blos - som__ time,
17
Cast their frag - rance on the__ air.
Ma - ples bright in Ta - tsu__ ta.
21
Spring is here for all to__ see.
Ka - ra - sa - ki's scent - ed__ pine.

1. Sakura, sakura
Yayoino sorawa
Miwatasu kagiri
Kasumi ka kumo ka
Nioi zo izura
Nioi zo izura
Mini yuka-n*

2. Saita sakura
Hana mite modoro
Tatsuta was momiji
Karasaki no matsu
Tokiwa tokiwa
Iza yuka-n*

* n is pronounced as a separate syllable.

THERE ONCE WAS A PUFFIN

ʳril Hampshire & others

*Cyril Hampshire (1900-1963)

Allegretto ♩ = 92-104

1. There once was a Puf-fin, Just the shape of a muf-fin, And he lived on an is-land In the bright_ blue_ sea! He ate lit-tle fish-es That were most de-li-cious, And he had them for sup-per and he had__ them for tea.

2. This cute lit-tle Puf-fin That_ looked like a muf-fin Tried to eat all the fish-ies In the bright_ blue_ sea! He got in-di-ges-tion! Of that there's no ques-tion. So he ate no more fish-ies for his sup-per and his tea.

MY VALENTINE

Anonymous

*Cyril Hampshir
(1900-1963

Smoothly ♩ = 84-92

mf

I have a lit-tle Val-en-tine that

mp

4

some-one sent to me, It's pink and white and red and blue and

6

pret-ty as can be: For-get-me-nots are round the edge and

8
poco rit.
ten.
a tempo
ti - ny ro - ses too, And such a love - ly piece of lace, The ve - ry pal - est blue; and
poco rit.
ten.
a tempo
11
in the cen - tre there's a heart as red as red can be, And
13
poco rit.
mf
broadly
on it's writ - ten all in gold "To you with love from me!"
poco rit.
mf
broadly

A COOKIE FOR SNIP

Margaret Hutchison

*Burton Kurt
(1890-1977

Playfully ♩ = 120-132

mf

Please! Please! May I have a cook-ie?

5

One for me and an-o-ther for Snip! Be-cause when I eat one__ a-lone, His

13
rall.
a tempo
mf
don't think just one cook - ie would hurt. Please! Please! May I have a cook - ie?
rall.
a tempo

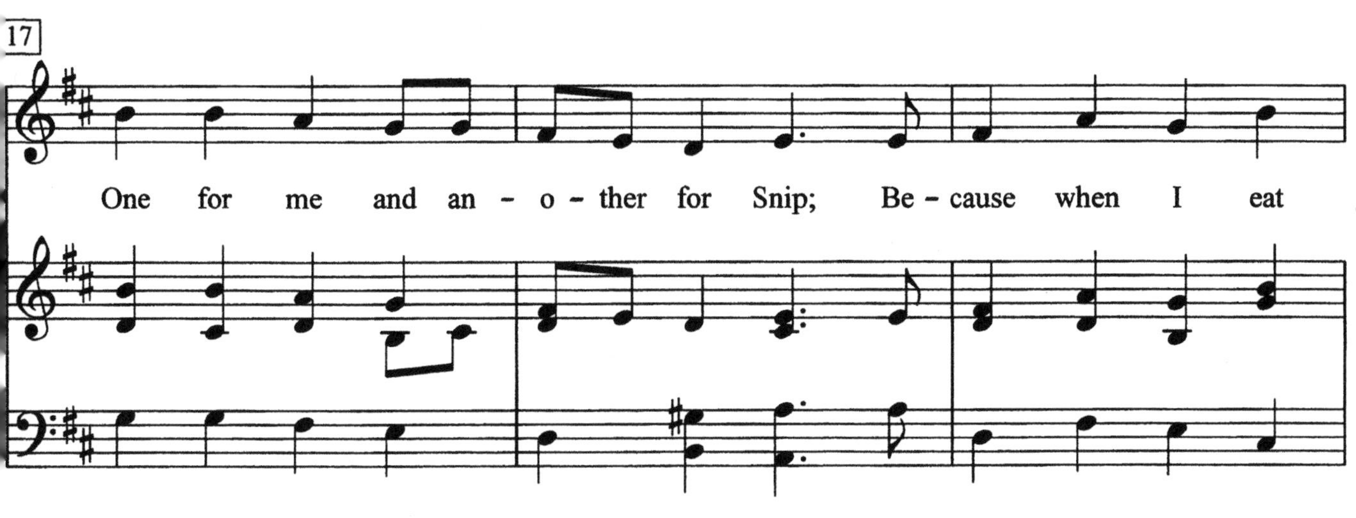
17
One for me and an - o - ther for Snip; Be - cause when I eat

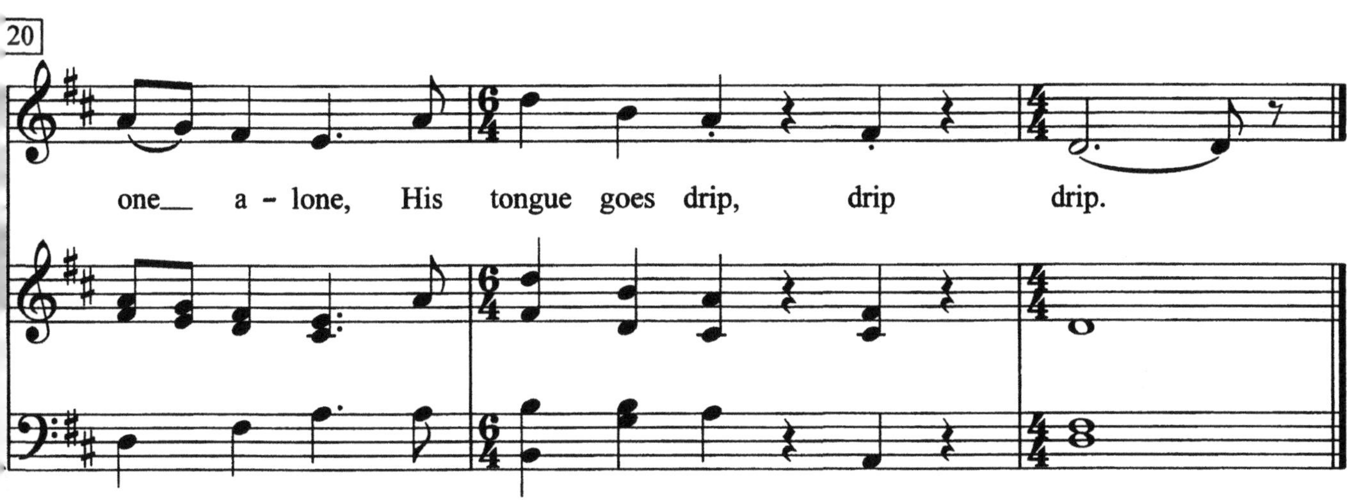
20
one__ a - lone, His tongue goes drip, drip drip.

DAISIES

Margaret Lyell

Margaret Lye
(1910-

With a lilt ♩. = 58-66

mp

1. Spring is here, the sky is blue, Gen - tle breez - es blow - ing. All a - bout the mea - dow green See the dai - sies grow - ing
2. When the sun is bright and warm Dai - sies lift their fa - ces. When the dark - ness falls, they hide, Deep in grass - y pla - ces.

mp

4

8

11
mf
rit. (2nd time only)
I know just what I will do Make a dai - sy
Fast a - sleep till morn - ing light, Pret - ty flow - ers good-
mf
rit. (2nd time only)
14
1.
chain for you.
night, good -
1.
18
rit.
2.
night.
2.
pp
rit.
rit.

ALMOST ASLEEP

David Ouchterlony

*David Ouchterlony
(1914-1987)

15
send you our love, and our watch we'll keep",
hard to find (four bar yawn),
21
p
rit. (2nd time only)
1.
When I'm al - most a - sleep.
When I'm al - most a -
rit. (2nd time only)
27
2.
sleep.
pp

IF I WERE...

Elizabeth Pollmer

*Elizabeth Pollme[r]
(1918-

Lively 𝅗𝅥. = 66-72

mf *mp*

5

1. If I were a bird I would sit in a tree, And lis - ten all day To the bum - ble - bee. If I were a

(2.) If I were a horse I would gal - lop a - way, Roam o - ver the prai - rie By night and day, If I were a

(3.) If I were a fish I would swim in the sea, And look at the boats sail - ing o - ver me, But I'm not a

10

14
bird I would sit in a tree. But I'm not a
horse I would gal - lop a - way, But I'm not a
fish I can't swim in the sea, I swim in the
18
rit.
a tempo
bird. I'm a child, as you see.
horse. I'm a child and I play.
bath tub, That's bet - ter for me.
rit.
a tempo
mf
22
1., 2.
3.
2. If
3. If
senza rit.
mp

PEAR-TREE AND PLUM-TREE

Doris Rowley

Alec Rowle
(1892-195

Simply ♩ = 100-108

mp

Pear – tree and Plum – tree, full of white

mp

8

mf

blos – som, What will you give us for wee ba – by May?_ A sha – dow to sit in, a

mf

15

poco rit. *a tempo*

wreath for her head, And a bird – ie to sing to her, all the long day.

mp *rit.* *poco rit.* *mp* *a tempo*

22
mp
Pear - tree and Plum - tree full of white blos - som,
pp
mp
29
mf
What will you give us for wee ba - by May?__ Ripe fruit to eat, and a
mf
35
rit.
dear lit - tle stone To plant in the gar - den, and keep for her own.
rit.
pp

EARTH

Shirley M. Shaw

*Marshall L. Shaw (1960-

1
mp
Soon you will see the gold - en grain. This will be food to
All our friends will be safe and free. And we can live in
Let this dream be our great - est quest. A hav - en of love and
mp
14
1., 2.
share with you and me.
true har - mo - ny.
peace for you and
1., 2.
17
3.
me.
3.
pp

SNOWY FLAKES

Frances B. Wood

Polish Caro[l]
arr. D. F. Coo[k]

Cantabile ♩ = 66-72

mp

1. Snow - y flakes are fal - ling soft - ly, Cloth - ing all the world in white. High a - bove the stars are shi - ning, Twink - ling through the win - try

(2) spread the won - drous sto - ry, "Je - sus Christ is born to - day. Peace on earth", they sang and "Glo - ry be to God on high al -

4

7

10
poco accel.
night.___ Was it just like this we won - der, Star - ry
way."___ So we sing our sweet - est ca - rols, Tell - ing
poco accel.
cresc.
13
f
a tempo
bright and crisp and cold, On that Christ - mas night of
how the God of love Came to earth from heav'n a -
f
a tempo
16
mp
1.
2.
old? 2. An - gels
bove.
p
mp
p
p

GLOSSARY

Compiled by Debra Wanless

About the Composers in Grade One

***ANDERSON, William Henry** (1882-1955). Canada. Anderson was born in England, and studied in London where he sang in several church choirs and with an opera company. Chronic bronchitis ended his career as a vocal soloist and he decided to seek a less humid climate. He emigrated to Canada in 1910, settling in Winnipeg, Manitoba where he worked as a voice teacher, choir director and composer. He composed more than 150 songs and approximately 40 church anthems.

***ARCHER, Violet** (born 1913). Canada.

Born in Montréal, Québec, Dr. Archer studied first at McGill University and then with Béla Bartók and Paul Hindemith. She taught at several universities in the United States before moving to the University of Alberta in Edmonton where she spent a long career as a teacher and composer. She is now retired, and lives in Ottawa, Ontario. Dr. Archer is a Member of the Order of Canada, and also was awarded Composer of the Year in 1984. She has composed works for orchestra, choir, solo organ, voice, and piano.

***BELYEA, W. Herbert** (born 1917).

Canada. Born in Winnipeg, Manitoba, Belyea received his early training with the Winnipeg Boys' Choir and the All Saints Anglican Church Choir. W. H. Anderson was one of Belyea's teachers. Belyea's musical career was interrupted while he served in the Canadian Army during World War II. He returned to Canada after the war, and completed his studies at the University of Manitoba where he later taught.

BRACE, Geoffrey. Britain. Nothing is known of him except that he was an arranger of numerous songs.

***BROUGHTON, Marilyn E.** (born

1940). Canada. Born in Toronto, Ontario, Broughton studied at the Trinity College of Music and the University of Toronto. She worked for seven years as a high school mathematics teacher before leaving to raise a family. Today, she lives in Toronto where she sings in several choirs, is active as a piano accompanist, and composes music for young people.

***COOK, Donald F.** (born 1937). Canada. Cook grew up and received his

early music training in St. John's, Newfoundland. After further studies in New York City and London, England, Dr. Cook returned to Newfoundland in 1967 to become the founding director of the School of Music at Memorial University. Since 1992, he has served as Principal of Western Ontario Conservatory (now Conservatory Canada). Most of his compositions are for solo voice or choir, and many are based on Canadian folk songs.

***CRAWLEY, Clifford** (born 1929). Canada. Born and educated in England, where he studied with composers Lennox Berkeley and Humphrey Searle, Crawley taught music in elementary and secondary schools before emigrating to Canada in 1973. He is a Professor Emeritus of Queen's University in Kingston, Ontario, where he taught from 1973 to 1993. He now resides in Toronto where he continues to compose and work as a music consultant, choir director, adjudicator, and examiner. Crawley has written more than 80 compositions, at times using the pen name Clifford Curwin. His works, many of which are intended for young players, include piano duets, operas, chamber works, and many pieces for band, orchestra and choir. Crawley is an active participant in the "Creating Music in the Classroom" and "Artists in the Schools" programs in Ontario.

DUNHILL, Thomas Frederick (1877-1946). Britain. Dunhill grew up in London and received his music training at the Royal College of Music where he studied composition with Sir Charles Stanford. As a young man, Dunhill served as assistant music master at the famous boys' school, Eton College. He later taught at the Royal College of Music in London, and spent more of his time composing. He wrote some chamber music, two light operas and two ballets. He wrote charming songs, many of them for children, as well as children's cantatas, operettas, and other works intended for educational purposes.

DURING, Camilla (20th century). Britain. Little is known about During except that she published a set of songs in 1995.

***FIELDER, Steven** (born 1950). Canada. Born and raised in Toronto, Ontario, Fielder graduated from the University of Waterloo and The University of Western Ontario. He currently maintains an active teaching studio at Conservatory Canada (London, Ontario), and also serves as an examiner for piano and theory. Fielder is the author of *Keyboard Harmony & Transposition* and Conservatory Canada's Theory textbooks for Grades 1 to 4.

***FLEMING, Gordon** (1903-1959). Canada. Fleming was born in Goderich, Ontario. He began studying music in 1916, and played professionally in theatres and churches, concert halls and on the radio. He moved to Windsor, Ontario in 1929 where he spent the remainder of his life. He composed symphonic pieces, film scores, and piano and vocal works, many of which were commissioned by the CBC.

***HAMPSHIRE, Cyril** (1900-1963). Canada. Hampshire was a pianist, choir conductor, adjudicator and composer born in Wakefield, England. He was an assistant organist at the age of 14, and studied at Leeds College. Hampshire came to Canada in 1921, and lived for a time in Moose Jaw, Saskatchewan. In 1939 he became Principal of the Hamilton Conservatory of Music in Hamilton, Ontario. Six years later, he accepted an appointment as director of music for the Hamilton public schools. It is therefore not surprising that he composed and arranged songs for school children, and also compiled the useful book *An Introduction to Practical Sight Singing*, published in 1951.

***KURTH, Burton** (1890-1977). Canada.

Kurth was a singer, educator, composer and organist who was born in Buffalo, New York. He studied in New York, Winnipeg and Chicago, settling in Winnipeg in 1909 to teach singing. He moved to Vancouver in 1927 where he had a long career as church organist and supervisor of music for Vancouver schools. Kurth composed many songs for use in schools and also compiled several collections including *Little Songs for Little People*, *Music Makers*, and *Sing Me a Song*. His book *Sensitive Singing* offers advice to young singers.

LYELL, Margaret (born 1910). Britain. Born in Perth, Scotland, Lyell studied at the Royal Academy of Music in London on a Carnegie grant in 1928 and later studied in Berlin. She works in England as a composer, editor, arranger, and translator. Her compositions include pieces for string quartet, piano, and violin. Lyell also wrote children's songs including *Four Little Songs for Little People.*

***OUCHTERLONY, David** (1914-1987).

Canada. Dr. Ouchterlony was born in Guelph, Ontario and was an organist, choirmaster, teacher, administrator and adjudicator. A pupil of Healey Willan, Dr. Ouchterlony taught at a number of private schools around Ontario before settling in Toronto to become a teacher at (and later Principal of) the Royal Conservatory. His works are mostly short vocal or instrumental pieces. His well-known *Carol Cantata*, which features carols in the styles of eight nations, was first performed in 1975 at Timothy Eaton Memorial Church (Toronto), where Dr. Ouchterlony was the organist and choirmaster.

***POLLMER, Elizabeth** (born 1918). Canada. Nothing else is known about this composer.

ROWLEY, Alec (1892-1958). Britain. Rowley was born in London and spent his entire career in that city. He studied at the Royal Academy of Music, winning prizes for both composition and piano. He was a fluent and original writer of songs, chamber music, and works for organ and piano. Much of his music is attractive and accessible to the young student.

***SHAW, Marshall** (born 1960). Canada. Shaw, originally from Toronto, Ontario, graduated with a degree in music from Queen's University in Kingston, Ontario. He remained there to play French horn with the Kingston Symphony Orchestra for 13 years, and to teach music in schools. During this time, he composed 12 children's songs set to poems by his mother, Shirley Shaw. These songs complement various subject areas taught in school. In recent years, Shaw has become highly involved in composition using computers and synthesizers.

***STEPHEN, Roberta** (born 1931). Canada. Born in Calgary, Alberta, Roberta Stephen is a graduate of the University of Calgary and the University of North Texas. She now lives in Calgary where she is active as a teacher, composer, and adjudicator. Her song cycles and children's instrumental music are performed across Canada and the United States. Stephen is also president of Alberta Keys Music Publishing Company.

GRADE ONE – EXAMINATION REQUIREMENTS

Length of the examination: 20 minutes

Examination Fee: Please consult the current examination application form for the schedule of fees.

Co-requisite: None. There is NO written examination co-requisite for the awarding of the Grade 1 Practical Certificate.

NOTE: The Grade 1 examination is designed for the younger beginner. It is recommended that mature beginners enter the examination program at the Grade 4 level.

Candidates are expected to know all of the requirements and regulations for the examination as outlined in the current Conservatory Canada Voice Syllabus. In the event of a discrepancy between the current syllabus and the requirements set out below, the Syllabus must be considered definitive for examination purposes. No allowance can be made for candidates who misread or fail to follow any of the regulations and/or requirements for the examinations.

REQUIREMENTS & MARKING

Requirement	*Total Marks*
THREE CONTRASTING PIECES Chosen from the List (16 marks each)	48
ONE SUPPLEMENTARY PIECE	8
VOCALISES: None required	0
TECHNICAL TESTS	16
SIGHT READING Rhythm Pattern Singing	 3 7
AURAL TESTS	10
VIVA VOCE	8
TOTAL POSSIBLE MARKS	100

NOTE: The examination program must include at least ONE piece by a Canadian composer. The Canadian piece may be chosen from the List Pieces OR as the Supplementary Piece.

PIECES

Candidates are required to perform THREE PIECES from the List, contrasting in key, tempo, mood, and subject. Your choices must include three different composers. All pieces must be sung from memory. Pieces may be transposed to suit the compass of the candidate's voice.

SUPPLEMENTARY PIECE

Candidates must be prepared to sing from memory ONE SUPPLEMENTARY PIECE. This piece need not be from the Syllabus list, and may be chosen entirely at the discretion of the teacher and student. It may represent a period or style of piece not already included in the examination program, but which holds special interest for the candidate. An unaccompanied folk song may be used. The choice must be within the following guidelines:

1) The equivalent level of difficulty of the piece may be at a higher level, providing it is within the technical and musical grasp of the candidate.
2) Pieces at the pre-Grade 1 level are acceptable.
3) The piece must be suitable for the candidate's voice and age.
4) The piece must be for solo voice (with or without piano accompaniment). Vocal duets are not acceptable.

Special approval is not required for the Supplementary Piece. However, poor suitability of choice may be reflected in the mark.

TECHNICAL EXERCISES

Candidates must be prepared to sing any or all of the exercises given below, in the following manner:

i) sung to vowels

Ah [*a*], ay [*e*], ee [*i*], oh [*o*], oo [*u*]

as requested by the examiner. Though the tonic sol-fa names may be used to learn these exercises, candidates may NOT sing using sol-fa names in the examination.

ii) sung without accompaniment. A starting pitch will be given by the examiner. Exercises may be transposed from the keys given below into keys suitable to the candidate's voice range. The examiner may give a different starting pitch for each exercise.

iii) metronome markings should be regarded as *minimum* speeds.

iv) expression markings are not given for Grade 1 and are NOT required for the examination.

v) all exercises must be sung in a single breath unless a breath mark is indicated in the score by a comma.

vi) A slur has been used to indicate legato singing. Staccato markings have been used to indicate staccato singing.

SIGHT READING

Candidates are required to perform at sight a) a rhythmic exercise and b) a passage of vocal score as described below. The candidate will be given a brief period to scan the score before beginning to sing. However, candidates are not permitted to hum the melody while scanning. Candidates must perform the rhythm section without counting aloud. It is recommended that candidates choose a moderate tempo, maintain a steady beat, and avoid the unnecessary repetition caused by attempting to correct errors during the performance.

Before the candidate attempts to sing the vocal passage, the Examiner will play on the piano a I-IV-V-I chord progression (with the leading-note to tonic in the upper part) to establish the key and tonality. The tonic note will then be given.

a) Rhythm	*b) Vocal Passage*
To tap, clap or play on one note (at the candidate's choice) a simple rhythm. Length 4 bars Time signature 2/4, 3/4 Note values 1/2, dotted 1/2, 1/4, 1/8 Rest values no rest values	To sing at sight a simple unaccompanied melody, within a range of five notes (*doh* to *soh*) and within the limits of the great (or grand) staff. The melody begins on the tonic note. Candidates may use either any vowel of their choice or the tonic sol-fa names. Major keys only C, F, G Length 4 bars Time signature 2/4, 3/4 Note values 1/2, dotted 1/2. 1/4 Rest values whole rests Melodic Intervals 2nds & 3rds only

AURAL TESTS

The candidate will be required:

i) to clap back the rhythmic pattern of a short melody, 4 bars in length, in 2/4 or 3/4 time, consisting of half, dotted half, quarter and eighth notes, after it has been played twice by the Examiner at the keyboard. Following is the approximate level of difficulty:

ii) to identify *major* or *minor* triad chords played once by the Examiner in broken form and in close, root position:

iii) the *major* common [four-note] chord of any key will be played once by the Examiner in broken form slowly, ascending and descending. The chord will be in root position. One of the four notes will then be re-sounded for the candidate to identify by saying, at the candidate's choice:
EITHER its interval number [1, 3, 5, 8], **OR** its tonic sol-fa name [doh, me, soh, upper doh].

VIVA VOCE

Candidates must be prepared to give verbal answers to questions on the THREE List pieces selected for the examination. Candidates must ensure that all teaching notes and other written comments are removed from the score before the examination. The questions will include the following elements:

i) to find and explain all of the signs (including clefs, time signatures, key signatures, accidentals, etc.), articulation markings (legato, staccato, accents, phrase or slur markings, etc.), dynamic and tempo markings, and other musical terms as they may be found in the three selected pieces.

ii) without reference to the score, to give the title, key and composer of the piece.

iii) to explain the meaning of the title of the piece.

iv) to find and play on the piano, any white key *within two octaves above or below middle C*, as requested by the Examiner. Candidates will not be required to read this note from score.

O CANADA

Written in French by Adolphe-Basile Routhier (1839-1920) in Quebec City and first performed there in 1880 to a musical setting by Calixa Lavallée. Translated into English in 1908 by Robert Stanley Wier (1856-1926). Approved as Canada's national anthem by the Parliament of Canada in 1967 and adopted officially in 1980.

Adolphe-Basile Routhier
English version by Robert Stanley Wier

*Calixa Lavall
(1842-189
arr. D.F. Coo

toire est un é - po - pé - e des plus bril - lants_ ex - ploits.
far and wide, O___ Ca - na - da, we stand on guard_for__ thee.
Et ta va - leur, de foi trem - pé - e,
God keep our land glo - rious and free;
pro - té - ge - ra nos foy - ers et nos droits,
O Ca - na - da, we stand on guard for thee.
pro - té - ge - ra nos foy - ers et nos droits.
O Ca - na - da, we stand on guard for thee.

Conservatory Canada conducts piano examinations throughout Canada from the Grade 1 level to the professional Associate Diploma level.

Please direct all examination enquiries to:

Office of the Registrar
Conservatory Canada
45 King Street, Suite 61
London, Ontario, Canada
N6A 1B8

Telephone: 519-433-3147
Toll free in Canada: 1-800-461-5367

Fax: 519-433-7404

Email: officeadmin@conservatorycanada.ca

For more information visit our website at:
www.conservatorycanada.ca